W9-AZM-420

TOP TEAMS

THE ROAD TO THE
WORLD'S MOST POPULAR
CUP:

HISTORY OF THE CUP

MAKING THE FINAL 32

TEAM USA

TOP TEAMS

WORLD STARS

THE ROAD TO THE
WORLD'S MOST POPULAR
CUP

TOP TEAMS

MASON CREST

MASON CREST

450 Parkway Drive, Suite D | Broomall, Pennsylvania 19008
(866) MCP-BOOK (toll-free)

Andrew Luke

First printing
9 8 7 6 5 4 3 2 1

ISBN (hardback) 978-1-4222-3951-3
ISBN (series) 978-1-4222-3949-0
ISBN (ebook) 978-1-4222-7829-1

Cataloging-in-Publication Data on file
with the Library of Congress

QR CODES AND LINKS TO THIRD-PARTY CONTENT

CONTENTS

KEY ICONS TO LOOK FOR:

Words to Understand: These words with their easy-to-understand definitions will increase the reader's understanding of the text while building vocabulary skills.

Sidebars: This boxed material within the main text allows readers to build knowledge, gain insights, explore possibilities, and broaden their perspectives by weaving together additional information to provide realistic and holistic perspectives.

Educational videos: Readers can view videos by scanning our QR codes, providing them with additional educational content to supplement the text. Examples include news coverage, moments in history, speeches, iconic sports moments, and much more!

Text-Dependent Questions: These questions send the reader back to the text for more careful attention to the evidence presented there.

Research Projects: Readers are pointed toward areas of further inquiry connected to each chapter. Suggestions are provided for projects that encourage deeper research and analysis.

Series Glossary of Key Terms: This back-of-the book glossary contains terminology used throughout this series. Words found here increase the reader's ability to read and comprehend higher-level books and articles in this field.

Aggregate: combined score of matches between two teams in a two-match (with each often referred to as "legs") format, typically with each team playing one home match.

Away goals rule: tie-breaker applied in some competitions with two-legged matches. In cases where the aggregate score is tied, the team that has scored more goals away from home is deemed the winner.

Cap: each appearance by a player for his national team is referred to as a cap, a reference to an old English tradition where players would all receive actual caps.

Challenge: common term for a tackle—the method of a player winning the ball from an opponent—executed when either running at, beside, or sliding at the opponent.

Clean sheet: referencing no marks being made on the score sheet, when a goalkeeper or team does not concede a single goal during a match; a shutout.

Derby: match between two, usually local, rivals; e.g., Chelsea and Arsenal, both of which play in London.

Dummy: skill move performed by a player receiving a pass from a teammate; the player receiving the ball will intentionally allow the ball to run by them to a teammate close by without touching it, momentarily confusing the opponent as to who is playing the ball.

Equalizer: goal that makes the score even or tied.

First touch: refers to the initial play on a ball received by a player.

Football: a widely used name for soccer. Can also refer to the ball.

Group of death: group in a cup competition that is unusually competitive because the number of strong teams in the group is greater than the number of qualifying places available for the next phase of the tournament.

Kit: soccer-specific clothing worn by players, consisting at the minimum of a shirt, shorts, socks, specialized footwear, and (for goalkeepers) specialized gloves.

Loan: when a player temporarily plays for a club other than the one they are currently contracted to. Such a loan may last from a few weeks to one or more seasons.

Marking: defensive strategy that is either executed man-to-man or by zone, where each player is responsible for a specific area on the pitch.

Match: another word for game.

One touch: style of play in which the ball is passed around quickly using just one touch.

One-two: skill move in which Player One passes the ball to Player Two and runs past the opponent, whereupon they immediately receive the ball back from Player Two in one movement. Also known as a *give-and-go*.

Pitch: playing surface for a game of soccer; usually a specially prepared grass field. Referred to in the Laws of the Game as the field of play.

Set piece: dead ball routine that the attacking team has specifically practiced, such as a free kick taken close to the opposing goal, or a corner kick.

Through-ball: pass from the attacking team that goes straight through the opposition's defense to a teammate who runs to the ball.

Touch line: markings along the side of the pitch, indicating the boundaries of the playing area. Throw-ins are taken from behind this line.

Youth system (academy): young players are contracted to the club and trained to a high standard with the hope that some will develop into professional players. Some clubs provide academic as well as soccer education.

Almost every country in the world today has a national soccer team. This team is the one that attempts to qualify for the World Cup tournament every four years. In almost every one of these countries, the national team is a tremendous source of national pride, and its exploits are closely followed.

In the vast majority of countries, however, just qualifying for the World Cup is a significant accomplishment. Most countries have never sent a team to the tournament. Many have qualified only a single time, like Jamaica in 1998, for example. That team never won a single match, or even scored a single goal, but is still revered in the country just for making it to France that year.

Then there are those countries where World Cup qualification is expected every four years, and not qualifying would be a national scandal. Fans book trips to the host nations well in advance of their team qualifying with the full expectation that they will be cheering them on come tournament time. In these countries, failing to qualify will likely get managers fired and the usual players left off future teams.

On the top rung of this ladder of expectations are the teams that not only expect to qualify every four years but also believe they should win the World Cup each and every time. These countries are World Cup royalty, and they produce some of the best players in the world. Not qualifying is not even a consideration. Failing to advance beyond the first round would be a travesty and result in people being fired. Anything less than a semifinals berth would be unacceptable, and not making the final match might well be considered a failure.

There are four countries that operate under this standard for every World Cup: Argentina, Brazil, Germany, and Italy. All have had at least five semifinal appearances and have won multiple World Cups. Most of the greatest matches in World Cup history involve at least one of these teams, and their players have produced some of the most memorable moments in the history of the sport.

deftly: skillfully or cleverly

flamboyant: marked by or given to strikingly elaborate or colorful display or behavior

partisan: strongly supporting something or someone

CHAPTER 1

ARGENTINA

It is not unusual to hear the expression "soccer is a religion" when referring to the sport in many South American countries. In Argentina, however, there are those who take that expression quite literally.

The Maradonian Church was founded in 2001 in Rosario, about a three-hour drive from the capital Buenos Aires. Followers of this church, who total more than 200,000, worship Argentine soccer icon Diego Maradona—or as they simply refer to him, El Diego. Maradona is the most famous and beloved figure in the rich history of Argentine soccer. The **flamboyant** midfielder casts a huge shadow, despite standing only 5'5". His followers' symbol for him is D10S, which combines his uniform number 10 with the Spanish word for God, Dios.

The worship of Maradona is just one example of the passion that soccer stirs in the hearts of the Argentine people. This passion is at peak level for the country's national team, nicknamed La Albiceleste, which means "the white and sky blue"—the uniform colors of the team.

The first match in national team history came against neighboring Uruguay in 1901. 29 years later, Argentina again played Uruguay in the final of the very first World Cup, a match it lost 4–2.

Diego Maradona is literally revered like a god in Argentina

It would be 48 years before Argentina would return to a World Cup final match. In 1978, the World Cup was played on Argentine soil, and there was great pressure on the team to improve on results that had seen it manage to advance to the quarterfinals just once since 1930. Only 16 teams qualified for the tournament in those days. Argentina drew into Group 1 with Italy, France, and Hungary. Led by captain Daniel Passarella at center back and attacking midfielder Mario Kempes, La Albiceleste went 2–1, losing only to Italy to finish second in the group.

In the second round, the remaining eight teams were again put in groups of four and played a round-robin. Argentina was grouped with Brazil, Poland, and Peru. Kempes, wearing the now iconic number 10 jersey for Argentina, was dominant in the first match against Poland, scoring his first two goals of the World Cup for a 2–0 win. Argentina's second match came against the formidable Brazilians, but neither team could breach the other's defense in a goalless draw.

On June 21st Brazil played Poland three hours before Argentina faced Peru in the final round-robin matches for all teams. With both Argentina and Brazil tied atop the group, if both won that day, the group would be decided by goal differential. Brazil came in at +3 to Argentina's +2. The Brazilians beat Poland as expected, by a score of 3–1. Therefore, Argentina knew it would need to outscore Peru by at least four goals to overcome Brazil's +5. Kempes scored twice, as did striker Leopoldo Luque. Luque's back-to-back markers made it 4–0 and 5–0, ensuring the group win for Argentina in a match that ended 6–0.

The win put Argentina in the final match against the other group winner, the Netherlands. The match was played in front of a wildly **partisan** crowd in Buenos Aires. Kempes struck first, scoring the only first-half goal. The match went deep into the second half before the Dutch tied it with just eight minutes left. The match went to 30 minutes of extra time, and 15 minutes in, Kempes struck again, beating two defenders and knocking in his own rebound after the keeper denied his first attempt. Ticker tape rained down from the stands as the crowd hit fever pitch. With the Dutch pressing for the equalizer, Argentina scored again 10 minutes later to seal the 3–1 victory and Argentina's first ever World Cup in front of its delirious fans. Kempes was named the Golden Boot winner with his six tournament goals.

Mario Kempes scored the World Cup-winning goal against the Netherlands in 1978

SIDEBAR: TOP 10 GOAL SCORERS IN ARGENTINA NATIONAL TEAM HISTORY

PLAYER	CAPS	GOALS
Lionel Messi*	118	58
Gabriel Batistuta	77	54
Hernán Crespo	64	35
Diego Maradona	91	34
Sergio Agüero*	82	34
Gonzalo Higuain*	68	31
Luis Artime	25	24
Daniel Passarella	70	23
Leopoldo Luque	45	22
José Sanfilippo	29	22

* - active

Argentina was defending champion in Spain in 1982 with Passerella and Kempes returning, but this Argentina squad featured 21-year-old phenom Maradona. As Argentina awards jersey numbers alphabetically, Maradona wore the number 10 jersey. With the World Cup now expanded to 24 teams, La Albiceleste opened with a 1–0 loss to Belgium, but in game two against Hungary, Maradona began to write his World Cup story. He scored twice, playing beside Kempes in a 4–1 win. Argentina then beat El Salvador to finish second in the group and advance.

The second round now had four groups of three teams, with only the group winners advancing. Argentina drew in with the powerful Brazilians and Italians, and lost both matches to end its tournament.

By 1986 in Mexico, Maradona was one of the world's best players and had been named captain of La Albiceleste. Kempes and Passarella had retired, and the fiery Maradona was the face of the team.

Argentina opened Group A play with an easy 3–1 win over South Korea. Match two was against defending champion Italy, and Maradona scored the goal in a 1–1 draw. A 2–0 win over Bulgaria gave Argentina the

Fillol

Olguin Galván Passarella Tarantini

Gallego Ardiles

Bertoni Maradona Kempes

Díaz

Czerniatynski Vandenbergh

Vercauteren Coeck Ceulemans Vandersmissen

De Schrijver Baecke Millecamps Gerets

Pfaff

*Argentina faced Belgium with Maradona in the lineup
for its opening match at the 1982 World Cup in Spain*

group, and it advanced to the second round, which was now a knockout stage rather than another round-robin. Argentina beat Uruguay to advance to the quarterfinal against England.

The match between England and Argentina is one of the most famous in World Cup history. The match came with a dramatic off-field backstory, as the two countries had been at war with each other just four years earlier in the Falkland Islands. Neither team managed to score in the first half, but the second saw two of the most famous goals in World Cup history—and in Maradona's career.

Maradona celebrates after scoring the Goal of the Century in the 1986 World Cup semifinals against England

At 51 minutes, an attacking Maradona cut down the middle of the defense and played the ball to the right at the top of the penalty area. Defender Steve Hodge tried to clear it but mishit the ball instead, sending it high in the air directly toward his keeper at the top of the six-yard box. Maradona had continued his run down the middle and was there to contest the ball with keeper Peter Shilton. Both men leapt into the air for it, but it was Maradona who connected with the ball, knocking it into the goal. What the referee failed to see, but which was clear on replays, was that Maradona had hit the ball with his left hand. Defender Terry Fenwick was just feet away and called for the handball immediately. When the call did not come, he ran to argue with the referee as Maradona and Argentina celebrated. The goal stood, and Maradona later declared that the goal was scored "a little with the head of Maradona and a little with the hand of God."

Just four minutes after the infamous Hand of God goal, the shell-shocked English allowed Maradona to score the perfectly legal Goal of the Century. Maradona received a pass in his own half about 10 yards from the center line. He **deftly** beat two English players to break across center on the right side of the pitch. Five seconds after getting the ball, he was in full sprint. Approached by defender Terry Butcher, Maradona feinted to the outside and then deked Butcher by cutting back inside. His next obstacle as he approached the penalty area was Fenwick, who was flat footed and easily evaded by the onrushing Maradona. In alone against the keeper now, who was running out to challenge him, Maradona gave him the same treatment that he did to Fenwick, beating Shilton to the outside and guiding the ball into the empty goal from six yards out. Many players and experts have declared Maradona's 12-second run of brilliance to be the best individual goal ever scored. The English managed to recover and score a late goal, but could not equalize and lost 2–1.

In the semifinal, Maradona continued his rampage against opposing defenders, scoring both Argentina goals against Belgium in another 2–0 victory to advance to the final against West Germany.

In the final, the Germans trailed 2–0 approaching the 74th minute, when they struck for two goals in seven minutes to tie the match. Just three minutes later, Maradona demonstrated his brilliance once again, spotting Jorge Burruchaga running into space. Maradona's perfect pass resulted in a breakaway and the World Cup-winning goal. Maradona was awarded the Golden Ball as the tournament's best player.

Diego Maradona scores the Goal of the Century and the announcer loves it

Maradona and Argentina were World Cup champions in 1986 after defeating Germany 3–2

At the next World Cup in Italy in 1990, Maradona again led his team to the final match. Argentina was fortunate to survive the group stage with just three points, but wins against Brazil, Yugoslavia, and Italy put them through to the final against West Germany. The Germans dominated the match, and Argentina managed just one shot on goal. The match was decided on a late penalty call against Roberto Sensini, and Argentina lost 1–0.

It would take another 24 years and the emergence of another Argentine superstar before Argentina challenged for the World Cup title again. In 2014 in Brazil, Lionel Messi, who had been named FIFA's best player in the world in three of the previous four years, led Argentina. La Albiceleste went unbeaten in group play, with Messi scoring four

There was no divine intervention for Maradona and Argentina in 1990 when they lost the final rematch to Germany

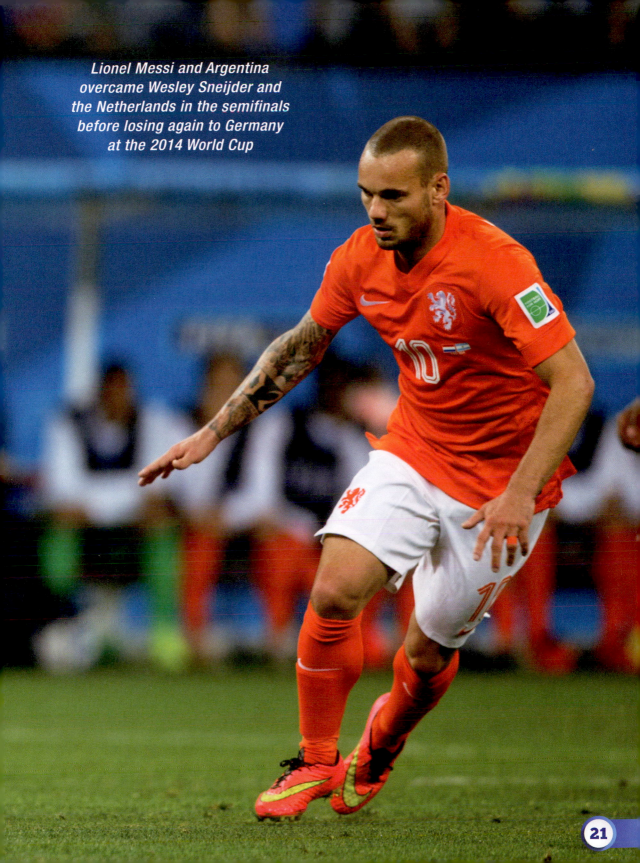

Lionel Messi and Argentina overcame Wesley Sneijder and the Netherlands in the semifinals before losing again to Germany at the 2014 World Cup

times in the three victories. Argentina then posted consecutive 1–0 wins over Switzerland and Belgium before beating the Netherlands in a penalty shootout to reach the final.

There, Argentina again found the Germans, who pulled out a very tight match with a goal 23 minutes into extra time. The 1–0 loss represented Argentina's third runner-up finish at the World Cup, to go along with 1930 and 1990. With World Cup wins in 1978 and 1986, Argentina is one of only four countries to reach the World Cup final five times. No other country has reached more than three. With Messi still at the top of his form and Argentina named 2016 FIFA Team of the Year, 2018 is looking promising for them.

TEXT-DEPENDENT QUESTIONS:

1. Where was the Maradonian Church founded?
2. Which two countries combined to eliminate Argentina at the 1982 World Cup?
3. Who won the Golden Ball award at the 1986 World Cup?

RESEARCH PROJECT:

Compare and contrast the careers of Diego Maradona and Lionel Messi, and based on the evidence you find, determine which player is better and write a report explaining why. Be sure to go beyond statistics to include each player's overall and team accomplishments, impact on the sport, and influence on Argentine culture.

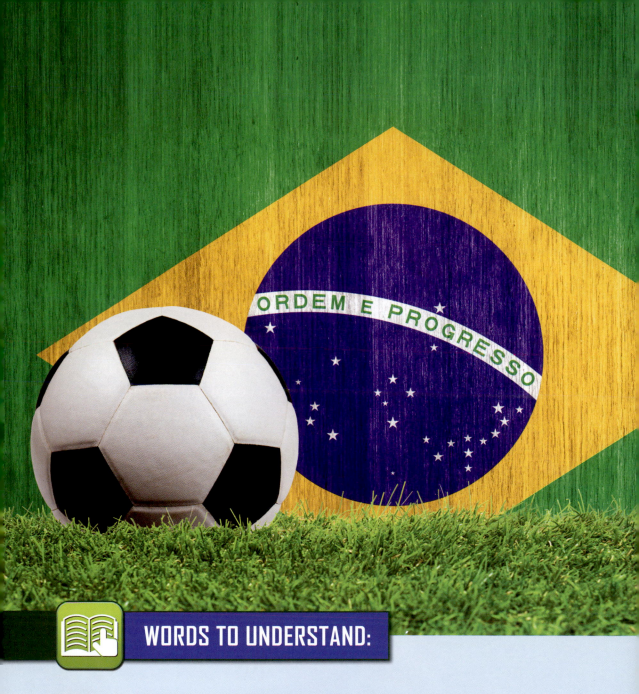

brazen: marked by shameless or disrespectful boldness

fervent: exhibiting or marked by great intensity of feeling

formidable: having qualities that discourage approach or attack

CHAPTER 2

BRAZIL

No other nation has had as much success at the World Cup as Brazil, which has participated in every World Cup tournament. It is hard to say whether this run of excellence has driven expectations, or if it is the other way around, but either way, Brazilians take their soccer very seriously. In some instances, they take it much too seriously.

The British brought the sport to Brazil in the late 1800s, and it grew to become a key fixture of the national culture in Brazil. In a few short decades, soccer was not only the undisputed pastime of the country but its heartfelt passion as well. In Brazil the sport had taken on the personality of its people, who played it with a distinctive flair and **brazen** creativity.

FIFA chose Brazil to host the World Cup in 1950, and the host nation's team was the overwhelming favorite to win. As expected, Brazil advanced to the final for the first time ever to meet Uruguay. A win for Brazil's team, nicknamed the Seleção (the Selected), was so widely

Maracanã Stadium opened at the beginning of the 1950 World Cup in Brazil, and is the site of the Maracanazo, the name given to Brazil's surprising defeat in the final

anticipated by the Brazilian people that several newspapers had already written stories of the victory before the match even started, and gold medals commemorating a Brazil victory were made.

But when the match was played, the Brazilians blew a 1–0 lead in the second half and lost 2–1. In the stands, three fans suffered heart attacks and died, and reports of fans committing suicide came from around the country.

There were no medals to present to Uruguay, as none had been made. There was no speech or ceremony, as FIFA president Jules Rimet had only written one congratulating Brazil. To this day, that match is called the Maracanazo (named for the stadium where it was played) and it is considered a national tragedy in Brazil. The team never again wore the colors they played in that day, white shirts with blue collars.

Redemption was eight years in coming for the Brazilians. After a quarterfinal exit in Switzerland in 1954, the Brazilians entered the competition in Sweden in 1958 with promise in the form of 16-year-old sensation Edson Arantes do Nascimento, better known simply as Pelé.

The young phenom had terrorized goalkeepers playing for Santos in Brazil's top club league, leading Santos in scoring at 16. At the beginning of the World Cup, Pelé was recovering from a knee injury, but his teammates were able to get a win and a draw in the first two matches without him. He made his World Cup debut in the third match against the Soviet Union, a 2–0 win to give Brazil the group.

In the knockout stage, Pelé made his impact. He scored the only goal of the match to eliminate Wales in the quarterfinals, and scored a second-half hat trick to secure victory over France in the semifinals. The opponent in the final match was host nation Sweden. With Brazil leading the Swedes 2–1 in the second half, Pelé scored the important third goal for Brazil, and added the team's final goal of the tournament in the 90th minute of the 5–2 win.

The Seleção triumph was monumental in Brazil. A spontaneous celebration erupted in city streets across the country, followed by more official parades and a presidential reception.

SIDEBAR: PLAYERS WITH THE MOST CAPS IN BRAZIL HISTORY

PLAYER	CAPS	LAST CAP
Cafu	142	2006
Roberto Carlos	125	2006
Lúcio	105	2011
Claudio Taffarel	101	1998
Robinho*	100	2017
Dani Alves*	100	2017
Djalma Santos	98	1968
Ronaldo	98	2011
Ronaldinho	97	2013
Gilmar	94	1969

* - active

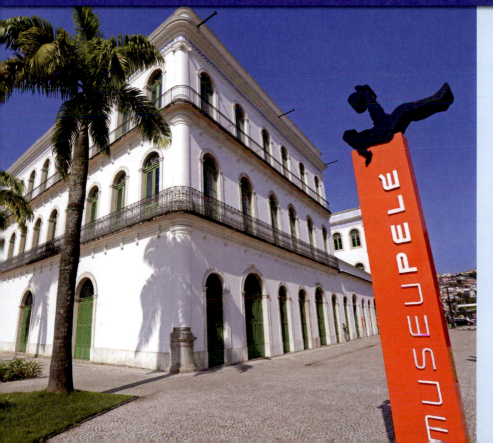

The Pelé Museum opened in 2014 in Santos, 56 years after Pelé made his World Cup debut with Brazil's 1958 championship team

Noted Brazilian anthropologist José Leite Lopes remembers the victory distinctly: "It was so intense. I don't think I was ever more moved by a few minutes of football in all my life. It was football's turning point."

The triumph only served to deepen the already **fervent** passion for the sport in Brazil, and legitimized the unstructured, free-flowing, and exciting soccer that had become Brazil's brand.

The 1962 tournament was held in Chile, where Pelé was injured in the team's second game and was lost for the tournament. This is when the quality of this Brazilian team shone through, as players like Garrincha and Vavá led the Seleção to the final again. Brazil won the match 3–1 over Czechoslovakia to claim back-to-back World Cups.

This postage stamp commemorates Brazil's victory in the 1962 World Cup

Injury once again came into play for Brazil during the 1966 World Cup in England. Brazil drew into Group 3 with Portugal, Hungary, and Bulgaria. From the opening match against the Bulgarians, it was clear that the strategy for Brazil's opponents was to foul Pelé hard. He scored once in the 2–0 victory over Bulgaria, but took such a beating that he was unable to play the next match against Hungary. Brazil lost 3–1, forcing Pelé into service for a must-win against Portugal. The Portuguese fouled Pelé mercilessly, aggravating his injury and preventing him from being effective in any way. Brazil lost 3–1 and was eliminated.

Soured by his experience in England, Pelé was reluctant to play for Brazil at the 1970 World Cup in Mexico. When he finally did agree to play, his addition formed what most experts believe is the best soccer team of

Pagliuca

Mussi — Baresi — Maldini — Benarrivo

Berti — D. Baggio — Albertini — Donadoni

R. Baggio — Massaro

Bebeto — Romario

Zinho — Mazinho

Dunga — Mauro Silva

Branco — Marcio Santos — Aldair — Jorginho

Taffarel

Although no goals were scored in the final match against Italy, Romário and Bebeto were a lethal combination up front for Brazil's 1994 World Cup winners

all time. Along with Pelé, this squad featured two players who would go on to eventually join Pelé among the top 10 scorers in Brazil history: Jairzinho and Tostão. With Gérson patrolling midfield and captain Carlos Alberto Torres anchoring the defense, the Brazilians were **formidable.**

Brazil drew into Group 3 and opened against Czechoslovakia. After falling behind 1–0 early, goals from Rivelino, Pelé, and a pair of goals from Jairzinho gave the Seleção a 4–1 win. Jairzinho scored again as Brazil shut out England 1–0 in the next match. Brazil wrapped up the group stage with a 3–2 win over Romania behind another Jairzinho goal and a pair from Pelé. Brazil won the group and advanced to face Peru in the quarterfinals.

In the quarterfinals, it was Tostão's turn to shine as he scored twice, adding to goals from Rivelino and Jairzinho for the 4–2 win. Brazil's semifinal opponent was rival Uruguay. After an even first half ended 1–1, Brazil's skill dominated the second half, as Jairzinho scored for the fifth straight game and Rivelino added a late goal in the 3–1 win.

Watch the highlights of the 1970 World Cup final match

Pelé opened the scoring in the final against Italy with a header 18 minutes in. The Italians equalized near the end of the half but continued to play a conservative defensive system. In the second half, the superior

Brazilian talent broke that system down, resulting in goals by Gérson, Carlos Alberto, and, of course, Jairzinho. Pelé assisted the last two. The Brazilians were champions again, and Pelé became the only player to be a three-time World Cup winner.

By winning three of the last four World Cups, Brazil established itself as the supreme power in world soccer. Pelé, however, retired from international play the next year, and it would be nearly a quarter century before Brazil reached the final match at a World Cup again.

BRAZIL

WORLD CUPS – 5

RUNNER UP – 2

BEST PLAYER

1970 – Pelé (4 goals)

1970
BEST TEAM

ITALY

WORLD CUPS – 4

RUNNER UP – 2

BEST PLAYER

1938 – Silvio Piola (5 goals)

1938
BEST TEAM

SUCCESSFUL WORLD CUP COUNTRIES

GERMANY

WORLD CUPS – 4

RUNNER UP – 4

BEST PLAYER

1990 – Lothar Matthäus (4 goals)

1990
BEST TEAM

ARGENTINA

WORLD CUPS – 2

RUNNER UP – 3

BEST PLAYER

1986 – Diego Maradona (5 goals)

1986
BEST TEAM

In 1994 Brazil drew into Group B, led by the captain Raí in midfield and Romário and Bebeto up front. Raí and Romário both scored in the 2–0 Seleção win over Russia to open Brazil's tournament in Palo Alto, California. In match two, Romário and Bebeto provided two of the three goals in a shutout of Cameroon, and Brazil wrapped up the group stage with a 1–1 draw with Sweden on yet another Romário goal.

In the knockout stage, Brazil faced the home side USA at Stanford Stadium in California. It was a tight match until Bebeto scored in the 73rd minute to win it for Brazil. Romário and Bebeto both scored again in the quarterfinal against the Netherlands, but it was Branco who scored the winner with less than 10 minutes to play for a thrilling 3–2 victory. The semifinals pit Brazil against the Swedes again, resulting in another tight match. This time, Romário was the hero with a late goal off a stellar one-two play in a 1–0 win.

Brazil faced the powerful Italians led by Roberto Baggio in the final match. The teams played cautiously, navigating their way through regulation and extra time without a single goal. For the first time, a World Cup final match went to a shootout, which Brazil won when Italy's top scorer Baggio missed his kick. Romário won the Golden Ball as the best player.

Eight years later, Brazil won a record fifth World Cup at the tournament in Korea and Japan. Brazil had an easy draw in Group C, beating Turkey, China, and Costa Rica. Ronaldo (Ronaldo Luís Nazário de Lima—not Cristiano Ronaldo, who was just 17 in 2002) scored four goals to lead the offense for Brazil. Ronaldo continued his brilliance in the knockout stage, scoring once against Belgium in the first knockout match, then again against Turkey in the semifinals, where he potted the match winner.

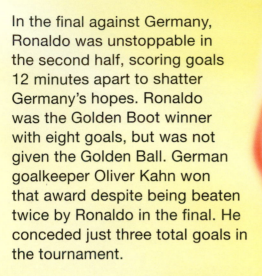

In the final against Germany, Ronaldo was unstoppable in the second half, scoring goals 12 minutes apart to shatter Germany's hopes. Ronaldo was the Golden Boot winner with eight goals, but was not given the Golden Ball. German goalkeeper Oliver Kahn won that award despite being beaten twice by Ronaldo in the final. He conceded just three total goals in the tournament.

The celebrations in Brazil were just as big as they were in 1958, 1962, 1970, and 1994. Brazilian style had overcome German precision to claim a fifth title, but Germany would continue to show just how successful its brand of soccer could be.

1. Which country hosted the World Cup in 1950?
2. Who won the Golden Ball at the 1994 World Cup?
3. Name four players on Brazil's 1970 World Cup team.

 RESEARCH PROJECT:

You will have noticed throughout this chapter that most of Brazil's star players, such as Pelé, Romário, and Ronaldo, go by only one name. Research and write a short report on the reason for this tradition, explaining not only why it is done but also where the names come from.

legacy: something (such as memories or knowledge) that comes from the past or from a person of the past

stifled: stopped (someone) from doing or expressing something; make something difficult or impossible

upstart: one that has risen suddenly (as from a low position to wealth or power)

GERMANY

No team in history has reached more World Cup finals than Germany. This is true despite the fact that Germany did not play in two World Cup tournaments: 1930, due to the expense of traveling to South America, and 1950, when it was banned from competition for political reasons following World War II. The ban was lifted for the 1954 tournament in Switzerland, and the Germans took full advantage of the invitation.

Coming off the ban on international competition, the country known post-WWII as West Germany qualified under the unusual format of the 1954 tournament as an unseeded team. It drew into a group with two seeded teams, a powerhouse from Hungary and Turkey. The Germans opened against Turkey and won easily, 4–1. Next up were the Hungarians, led by superstar Ferenc Puskás and Sándor Kocsis. The Hungarians embarrassed West Germany 8–3, and the Turks beat the winless South Koreans, forcing a group-stage playoff rematch between West Germany and Turkey. The Germans won even more decisively behind a hat trick from Max Morlock, 7–2.

West Germany advanced to the quarterfinals in the group runner-up bracket, where it shut out Yugoslavia 2–0, then demolished Austria 6–1 in the semifinals. This setup a rematch with the mighty Hungarians, who had come through the group winner bracket with two tough wins over Brazil and Uruguay without an injured Puskás. Kocsis was on a tear, having already scored a then-record 11 goals in the tournament.

With a five-goal win over the Germans already in the books earlier in the tournament, the Hungarians were expected to win the final easily. The Hungarians had won 31 straight matches coming into the World Cup, and were the reigning Olympic champions. Puskás returned to the Hungary lineup for the final.

The match was played in a heavy downpour in Bern, but that did not

ANGLIA - MAGYARORSZAG
1:7 LANTOS PUSKAS KOCSIS
KOCSIS TOTH HIDEGKUTI
BROADIS PUSKAS

In the 1954 final, West Germany upset Hungary, who had won more than 30 straight matches going into the World Cup, including this well-attended 7–1 drubbing of England

slow Hungary from bursting into the lead, scoring twice in the first eight minutes with goals from Puskás and Zoltán Czibor. West Germany countered, however, by scoring two of its own in just eight minutes, starting with Morlock's sixth of the tournament. Helmut Rahn then converted a corner kick at 18 minutes to tie the score. The match then settled down, and it was not until late in the second half that Rahn would prove to be the hero, scoring on a low, hard shot just inside the penalty area to give the Germans their first World Cup trophy.

Over the next four World Cups, West Germany fielded very competitive teams, finishing fourth, seventh, second, and third, respectively. In 1974, the tournament was held in West Germany, and the home side was determined to win.

Germany qualified teams from both East and West Germany for this tournament, and both drew into Group 1 with Chile and Australia. In the round-robin format, the Australians and Chileans scored just one goal between them in five matches, meaning that both German sides had already advanced to the next round when the teams met in the final match in Group 1. Though it had little meaning in the tournament, this World Cup meeting between the two political rivals was a tense one. The **upstart** East Germans beat their counterparts from the West 1–0.

In the second round, formatted as a two-group round-robin, the German teams were separated. West Germany made some adjustments to their alignment after the embarrassing loss to the East, and rolled through their second-round group, going 3–0 and giving up just two goals. Gerd Müller continued to lead the offense for West Germany, scoring his second and third goals of the tournament in that round. On the defense, captain Franz Beckenbauer was the anchor for the reigning European champions as they looked to add a World Cup title. Winning its second round group put West Germany in the final.

Check out Gerd Müller's winning goal from the 1974 World Cup

00:00

In the other second-round group, it was the Netherlands who went unbeaten behind their "Total Football" scheme and the brilliance of playmaking forward Johan Cruyff. In this Dutch scheme, players would rotate positions on the field as dictated by the flow of play, creating and filling space to confuse opponents and give its players more time when they had the ball.

Cruyff had scored three goals in the second round, but in the final, it was Beckenbauer and the Germans who **stifled** the Dutch attack. The first two goals of the match were scored on penalties in the first 25 minutes, one for each side. Just before halftime, Müller recovered after failing to handle a pass into his feet eight yards from the goal at the right post and fired the ball past the keeper toward the left post for a goal. That tally held up as the World Cup winner.

After bowing out in the second round at the 1978 World Cup in Argentina, West Germany went on a run of three straight World Cup final

The 1974 World Cup final match featured host country West Germany (in white) and the Netherlands

match appearances. They lost back-to-back finals matches in Spain in 1982 and Mexico in 1986. In 1990 in Italy, the Germans were finally able to turn the page.

Led by captain and World Cup veteran Lothar Matthäus and striker Jürgen Klinsmann, the Germans drew into Group D and opened against Yugoslavia. Matthäus scored twice and Klinsmann once in the 4–1 West Germany win. Both men also scored in the 5–1 win over the United Arab Emirates in match two. A draw against Colombia in the final group stage match was enough to clinch the group for the Germans, who advanced to face the Netherlands.

The Dutch had a strong team led by Frank Rijkaard, Marco van Basten, and Ruud Gullit, and were expected to give the Germans a battle. No goals were scored in the first half, but Klinsmann struck early in the second. With both sides playing with 10 men, Guido Buchwald made a run down the left side and crossed to an onrushing Klinsmann at the near post. He volleyed it past the keeper for the goal. Andreas Brehme scored a second goal five minutes from the end and West Germany hung on for the 2–1 win.

In the quarterfinals, a first-half Matthäus penalty kick produced the only goal of the match against Czechoslovakia, and the Germans needed penalty kicks to decide the semifinals against England in a match that was 1–1 after extra time.

In 2014, *Forbes Magazine* reported that the three highest-earning German players made more than the entire USA team national roster. With a consistently deep team that is always a threat to challenge for the World Cup title, it is no surprise that German players as a group are among the highest paid in the world. Here is a list of the wealthiest German players through the 2016–17 season, headed by former national captain Philip Lahm, who retired in 2017.

#	PLAYER	COUNTRY	CONTRACT VALUE ($)
1	Phillip Lahm	Bayern Munich	$100m
2	Bastian Schweinsteiger	Manchester United	$80m
3	Sami Khedira	Juventus	$60m
4	Marco Reus	Dortmund	$57m
5	Manuel Neuer	Bayern Munich	$52.8m
6	Mesut Özil	Arsenal	$50m
7	Matts Hummels	Bayern Munich	$40m
8	Lukas Poldolski	Galatasaray	$30m
9	Toni Kroos	Real Madrid	$29m
10	Miroslav Klose	Lazio	$25m

The final was a rematch of the final from the 1986 World Cup against Argentina and its superb superstar Diego Maradona. Argentina had triumphed 3–2 four years earlier, and the Germans were looking for revenge. Argentina was at a disadvantage to start, with four starters suspended due to accumulating yellow cards. The crowd in Rome was pro-German, and the match was an ugly one. Rough tackles on both sides went without being cautioned until midway through the second half. Substitute defender Pedro Monzón made a studs-up tackle on Klinsmann and was sent off.

West German captain Lothar Matthäus (L) celebrates with teammate Pierre Littbarski after winning the 1990 World Cup

With the defending champions down to 10 men and unable to generate any kind of attack, the Germans kept pressing. With just five minutes left, the referee called a tripping foul in the penalty area against Argentina, and Brehme scored to give West Germany the 1–0 win and its third World Cup trophy.

Yet another quarter century passed before Germany (the two Germanys unified after the 1990 World Cup) was able to add to its **legacy** again. The Germans had lost in the semifinals in the previous two World Cups, so they entered the 2014 tournament in Brazil looking to take that next step.

Always a favorite to win, Germany was ranked second in the world by FIFA behind only Spain. It drew into Group G and opened by humiliating Cristiano Ronaldo and an outgunned Portuguese team 4–0. Thomas

Defender Mats Hummels scored two goals for Germany at the 2014 World Cup

Müller scored a hat trick, Mats Hummels also scored, and Manuel Neuer kept a clean sheet in the win. The second match was a much tougher contest against a very game Ghana squad, resulting in a 2–2 draw. Germany advanced after Müller scored to give it a 1–0 win over the USA in the final group stage match.

Germany's first opponent in the knockout stage was Algeria, who gave the Germans a tough match, forcing them to extra time before Germany earned a 2–1 win. In the quarterfinals against France, an early goal by Hummels stood up for the 1–0 win, setting up a semifinal clash with the dynamic and dangerous hosts, the Brazilians.

Germany defeated Antoine Griezmann and France 1–0 in the 2014 World Cup quarterfinals

Brazil entered the match at a considerable disadvantage as they were missing two key players. Neymar was out due to injury and Thiago Silva was suspended for too many yellow cards. Brazil was unable to contend with the absence of these players and completely collapsed, allowing five goals in the first 30 minutes, including one from Müller and a pair from Toni Kroos. Germany scored two more in the second half as it cruised to a 7–1 thrashing of the embarrassed hosts.

This result pitted the Germans against Argentina for the third time in a World Cup final match. Rather than Maradona, this time the man to fear wearing the number 10 jersey was Lionel Messi, one of the best players

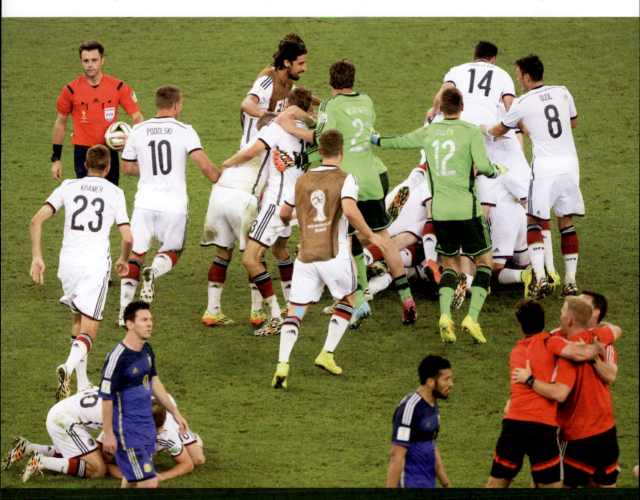

Argentina's Lionel Messi (bottom left, in blue) walks past dejectedly as German players celebrate their win in the final match of the 2014 World Cup in Brazil

in the world. Neuer and the German defense had been stout, however, allowing just four goals in the entire tournament, with three clean sheets. Neuer kept yet another clean sheet in the final against Messi and Argentina, as Germany scored an extra-time goal from Mario Götze to win its fourth World Cup.

Only Brazil has more World Cup trophies than the prolific Germans, who have finished in the top three a dozen times, more than anyone else. With typical German reliability, Germany has not finished worse than 7th in any World Cup since being allowed to compete again in 1954, and they have failed to reach the semifinals just 4 out of 16 times in that stretch.

TEXT-DEPENDENT QUESTIONS:

1. In which year was Germany banned from the World Cup?

2. What was the name of the scheme used by the Netherlands at the 1974 World Cup?

3. The absence of which two players gave Germany the advantage over Brazil in the 2014 World Cup semifinals?

RESEARCH PROJECT:

After World War II, Germany was divided into East and West Germany. Research the levels of success experienced by the soccer teams for each of these two countries. Outline the differences and give the reasons for them.

CHAPTER 4

ITALY

Italy has a rich and storied World Cup tradition, dating back to its first appearance as the hosts of the second-ever competition in 1934. And what a debut it was for Gli Azzurri, a nickname referencing the blue of the national team jerseys.

The national team first started competing in 1910, and by 1928 was good enough to win the bronze medal at the Summer Olympic Games in Amsterdam and the Central European International Cup in 1930.

Italy, like many European teams, declined to make the trip to Uruguay for the **inaugural** World Cup tournament. It was, however, one of two countries (along with Sweden) to bid for the tournament's second edition in 1934. FIFA's executive committee granted the Italians the tournament in 1932.

Italy won the bronze medal after beating Egypt 11–3 at the Olympic Stadium in Amsterdam in the 1928 Summer Olympic Games

As hosts, Italy made full use of its home advantage, opening the tournament before 25,000 adoring fans at Stadio Nazionale PNF in Rome. There was no round-robin in this early version of the World Cup, which was set up as a 16-team single-elimination tournament. Italy drew late qualifier the USA in that first match, and won easily 7–1 behind a hat trick from Angelo Schiavio. Spain presented a much tougher challenge in the quarterfinals.

The rough and tumble match ended in a 1–1 draw after extra time. One Italian player and the Spanish goalkeeper were each knocked out of the tournament with serious injuries. As the shootout had not yet been devised, if knockout-stage matches ended in a draw, they were replayed in their entirety.

In the replayed match held the next day, Italy's Guiseppe Meazza scored early and the Azzurri made that goal stand for the 1–0 win. In the semifinals against Austria, another early goal, by Enrique Guaita in the 19th minute, also stood up as the match winner for Italy.

*The 1934 Italian national soccer team
won the first of back-to-back World Cups in 1934*

The final in the second FIFA World Cup featured Czechoslovakia taking on the host Italians in front of a wildly partisan 55,000 fans. It was more than 100 degrees in Rome that day, and the match was sluggish through the first half. Czechoslovakia took the lead with a goal in the 71st minute, but Italy equalized 10 minutes later to force extra time. Just 5 minutes into extra time, it was Schiavio who found the net, and Italy held on for the 2–1 win.

The Azzurri continued to dominate the competition for the rest of the decade, defending the Central European International Cup title in 1935 and qualifying to defend the World Cup title in 1938 in France.

The Italian team started its World Cup defense in the single elimination knockout tournament against Norway in Marseilles. The Italians scored in the second minute but, dramatically, Norway equalized with just seven minutes remaining to force extra time. That is when Silvio Piola took over. Piola was a **prolific** scorer at both the club and international levels. He is the all-time leading goal scorer in the history of Italy's top division, Serie A. He also scored 30 international goals for Italy—third most of all time—in just 34 appearances. Against Norway, Piola scored four minutes into extra time to advance Italy to the quarterfinals.

The quarterfinal matchup was against none other than host France at the Stade Olympique de Colombes in Paris. Both teams scored in the first 10 minutes, and the score was 1–1 at the half. In the second half, Piola took over once more. The striker scored two goals to break the hearts of the 58,000 French fans in attendance, propelling Italy into the semifinals.

It was back to Marseilles for the semifinal match against Brazil, where neither team could score in the first half. Italy finally opened the scoring in the 51st minute, and then Meazza converted what would turn out to be a crucial penalty just nine minutes later. The penalty kick goal gave Italy the cushion to withstand a late Brazil goal and hold on to win 2–1.

In the final, Piola shone once again. The opponent was Hungary, and both teams scored in the first eight minutes. Goals from Piola and Gino Colaussi to close out the first half gave the Azzurri a 3–1 lead. Hungary scored in the 70th minute to get within a goal, but Piola put the match out of reach with his fifth goal of the tournament with just eight minutes remaining, and Italy claimed its second straight World Cup.

However, the next 32 years were a dark time for Italian soccer. In 1949, 10 national team players were killed in a plane crash. The Azzurri struggled to recover from this tragedy, failing to advance past the first round in four of the next five World Cups, and that fifth time, they failed even to qualify for the tournament. The program returned to glory in 1970, with a runner-up finish in Mexico. Italy had another strong showing in 1978, finishing fourth in Argentina, and setting the table for the 1982 World Cup in Spain.

On May 4, 1949, 10 members of the Italian national team were killed when a plane carrying the AC Torino club team crashed into an embankment

In 1982, the Italians were led by 40-year-old veteran captain and goalkeeper Dino Zoff and 25-year-old striker Paolo Rossi. The Azzurri drew into Group 1 in what was now a round-robin format in the first two rounds. The Italians played indifferently in the first round, and were lucky to advance after all three matches ended in draws.

The second round consisted of four three-team groups, and Italy was in the toughest one with Brazil and Argentina. Round two started against Argentina and neither team was able to produce a goal in the first half. In the second half, however, the Italians scored goals 10 minutes apart to take the lead, and held on to win 2–1.

Brazil also beat Argentina to eliminate them and set up a showdown to determine the group winner between Brazil and Italy. This match was Rossi's coming out party. Brazil had already scored 16 goals in winning all five of its matches, so Italy would need to find some scoring to match Brazil's firepower. Rossi did just that.

Paolo Rossi crushes the powerful Brazilians at the 1982 World Cup

00:00

Rossi wasted little time announcing his presence in the match, heading in a deep cross on the back post in the 5th minute. Team captain Sócrates equalized seven minutes later, but again it was Rossi who had an answer. He stole an **errant** pass by Toninho Cerezo and broke in alone on the keeper, beating him with a strike to the near side from the top of the penalty area. In the second half, Brazil pressed for the equalizer and was rewarded when Falcão struck with his left foot from the top of the area, beating Zoff to the far side. But once again, there was Rossi. Just six minutes after Falcão's goal, Italy took a corner kick on the right side. The ball deflected to Italy's Marco Tardelli, who managed a weak shot that took two bounces to Rossi in the six-yard box. The striker made no mistake in burying the ball in the back of the Brazilian goal for the hat trick.

Led by striker Paolo Rossi, Italy added a third World Cup championship in 1982

For an international soccer superpower, Italy does not traditionally score many goals. Luigi Riva is Italy's all-time leading goal scorer with a total of 35. That number would not even crack Germany's top 10. Italy's game is built around goalkeeping and defending, making stalwart defenders like Paolo Maldini and Fabio Cannavaro the stars, along with keepers like Gigi Buffon and Dino Zoff. So when an Italian scores a hat trick, it is a big deal. When he scores four goals in a match, it is a career highlight. Here is the list of four goal performances in Italian soccer history.

PLAYER	EVENT	OPPONENT
Carlo Biagi	1936 Summer Olympics	Japan
Francesco Pernigo	1948 Summer Olympics	USA
Omar Sivori	1962 FIFA World Cup qualifying	Israel
Alberto Orlando	Euro '64 qualifying	Turkey
Luigi Riva	1974 FIFA World Cup qualifying	Luxembourg
Roberto Bettega	1978 FIFA World Cup qualifying	Finland

The win propelled Rossi to superstardom and Italy to the semifinals against Poland, where Rossi was once again a one-man wrecking crew. In the first half, he scored on a free kick from just to the right side of the penalty area by running onto the ball in the six-yard box. Then Rossi put the game on ice in the second half when he headed in a beautiful chip from Bruno Conti.

West Germany was the opponent in the final, and the two teams battled to a 0–0 draw in the first half. Once again, it was Rossi who found the offense for Italy in the second half. Italy controlled the ball and had the Germans scrambling back off a quickly taken free kick. A cross came in from the right side and Rossi was there to knock it in at 57 minutes. Italy scored twice more before Germany scored a late goal to lose 3–1. Rossi

was a national hero after his Golden Boot- and Golden Ball-winning performance. He was named European and World Player of the Year.

The drought until Italy's next World Cup victory was not as long this time. Led by captain Fabio Cannavaro at center back, future captain goalkeeper Gianluigi Buffon, Andrea Pirlo in midfield, and Luca Toni upfront, Italy had a strong team going into the 2006 World Cup in Germany.

The 13th-ranked Italians drew into Group E for the 32-team tournament with Ghana, the USA, and the Czech Republic. Opening against Ghana, the Italians impressed. Pirlo scored by converting a corner kick with a shot from outside the top of the penalty area in the 40th minute. Substitute Vincenzo Iaquinta capitalized on a blunder by the Ghana defense to make it 2–0 in the second half, and Buffon kept a clean sheet for the win.

Against the USA, the Italian defense conceded a goal, but from an unlikely source. The match started well for the Italians when a Pirlo free kick found the head of Alberto Gilardino at the top of the six-yard box to open the scoring. But just five minutes later, defender Cristian Zaccardo misplayed a USA free kick to the back post. The ball came directly to him, but he mishit his clearing attempt and the ball went backward into the net for an own goal. The match ended 1–1.

The final group-stage match came against the Czechs. Substitute Marco Materazzi converted a corner kick in the first half. In the second half, with the Czechs pressing to equalize late but playing with just 10 men,

Italy had two players break in alone on the Czech goal, and another substitute, Filippo Inzaghi, scored to secure a 2–0 win.

Buffon kept a clean sheet to be named Man of the Match against Australia in a 1–0 win to open the knockout stage. He kept another clean sheet and Toni scored twice against Ukraine to win 3–0 in the quarterfinal.

The semifinal against Germany was filled with chances to score from both sides throughout regulation time. Both Buffon and German keeper Jens Lehman made great saves and several posts were hit. The match went to extra time at 0–0. In the 119th minute, Pirlo had an attempted clearance off a corner kick land at his feet, dribbled to his right to draw the defense to him, and slipped the ball through to Fabio Grosso in the penalty area, who scored to the far post. Italy added another goal two minutes later for the 2–0 win.

Goalkeeper Gianluigi Buffon and his Italian teammates were victorious at the 2006 World Cup in Germany

The opponent in the final match was France, who opened the scoring early off a penalty to Materazzi, which French captain Zinedine Zidane converted. Italy struck back midway through the half as a Pirlo corner kick found the head of Materazzi, who redeemed himself by burying it in the center of the goal. The match went to extra time tied at 1–1. Then 20 minutes in, one of the most extraordinary moments in World Cup history occurred.

Zidane was jogging back up the field past Materazzi when Materazzi said something to him. Zidane reacted by turning and driving the crown of his head into Materazzi's chest. The referee immediately showed Zidane a red card, making him unavailable not only for the remaining 10 minutes, but also for the penalty shootout. In the shootout, the Italians, including Pirlo, Materazzi, and Grosso, all made their kicks, while France's David Trezeguet missed his to give Italy its fourth championship.

Buffon won the Yashin Award as best goalkeeper, and joined Rossi, Schiavio, and Piola in the **pantheon** of Italian World Cup heroes.

TEXT-DEPENDENT QUESTIONS:

1. In which year did Italy's national team start competing?

2. Who won the Golden Ball at the 1982 World Cup?

3. Why did French captain Zinedine Zidane receive a red card in the 2006 World Cup final?

RESEARCH PROJECT:

Research and write a report on legendary Italian goalkeeper Dino Zoff. Look up his international statistics and results, and compare them against those of other Italian goalkeepers and all goalkeepers from other countries as well. Be sure to outline not only the length but also the quality of his career.

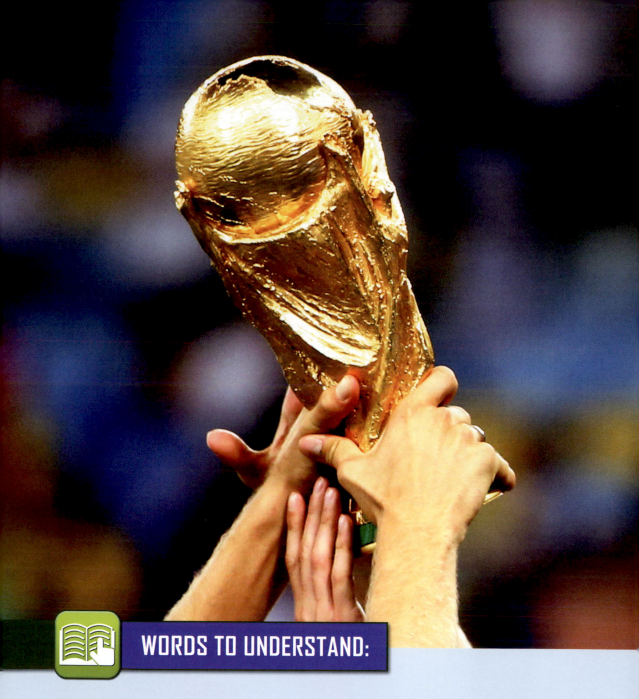

CHAPTER 5

BEST OF THE REST

Outside of Argentina, Brazil, Germany, and Italy, very few countries have found ultimate success at the World Cup. For some, glory has been **fleeting**. For others, it has remained just out of reach. And for still others, early success has faded before finally being rekindled in recent years.

For France, most successes have occurred in the last 35 years. Before this, however, was a magical run to the semifinals in 1958 in Sweden. Brazil was the champion that year behind the emergence of Pelé. But if

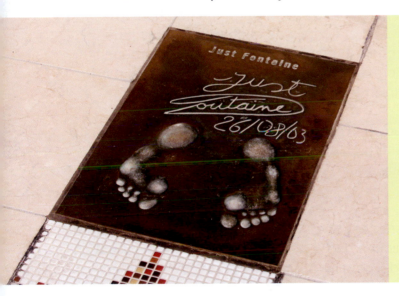

Just Fontaine's footprints on the Champion's Promenade in Montecarlo (Monaco), where there are various footprints of great champions of soccer. Fontaine still holds the record for most goals in a single World Cup, scoring 13 in 1958

there was a performance that outshone Pelé's at that tournament, it was that of French superstar Just Fontaine. Fontaine set the record for goals scored by a single player at a single World Cup tournament with 13. This included an opening-match hat trick versus Paraguay, and four goals in the third-place match against West Germany. When the two superstars met head-to-head, however, it was Pelé's star that shined brightest, outscoring Fontaine 3–1 in a 5–2 semifinal win to deny France its first appearance in the final match.

Michel Platini of France won the Ballon d'Or ("Golden Ball") as Europe's best player three straight times in the 1980s

France would not come close again until the 1980s, with teams led by dynamic captain Michel Platini. Platini won the Ballon d'Or ("Golden Ball") as European Player of the Year three straight times from 1983–85. In Spain in 1982 and Mexico in 1986, Platini was at the height of his powers as the best midfielder in the world.

In both tournaments, Platini led his team on runs to the semifinals. In both tournaments, the semifinal opponent was West Germany. The 1982 tournament saw Platini level the score at 1–1 with a penalty kick midway through the first half. The score was unchanged at full time. Each side scored a pair of goals in added extra time to force a penalty kick shootout, which the Germans won. The French then lost the third place match to Poland to finish fourth.

Buoyed by the promise shown in 1982, Platini and the French came into World Cup '86 in Mexico with high expectations. But in the semifinals, France lost to West Germany again. This time, France won its third-place match against Belgium.

Twelve years later, a different cast of characters filled the uniforms for Les Bleus, as the team is nicknamed. France qualified as the host nation, but was not highly regarded—coming in ranked 18th by FIFA. Didier Deschamps was the captain, yet the two biggest threats on the team were Zinedine Zidane and Thierry Henry. France drew into an easy group and went undefeated in the group stage. In the knockout stage, they needed extra time to beat Paraguay 1–0, and then Italy on penalty kicks after no goals were scored in 120 minutes.

In the semifinals, two goals from fullback Lilian Thuram defeated Croatia 2–1. That left the powerful Brazilians in the first-ever World Cup final match for France. Zidane opened the scoring, knocking in a corner kick with his head in the 27th minute. He closed out the first half the same way, scoring with a header from a corner on the opposite side. France added a second-half goal to win the World Cup 3–0, its first and only World Cup championship.

00:00

France won its first and only World Cup in 1998

France's most recent appearance in the final match came in 2006 in Germany, when Zidane, Thuram, and Henry were back for another run at the title. Despite losing to Italy and famously receiving a red card in the final, Zidane was named Golden Ball winner that year.

Like France, Uruguay has also made five semifinal appearances. That "other" South American champion won the very first event on home soil in Montevideo in 1930. Those early World Cup years were extremely successful for La Celeste, the national team. Along with the title in 1930 came another win 20 years later in Brazil. Uruguay did not enter the 1934 or 1938 events due to the difficulty of traveling to Europe. Óscar Miguez was the leader of the team in the 1950 tournament, scoring five goals. Uruguay came from behind in the semifinals against Sweden to win 3–2, and in the final match against Brazil to win 2–1. The win over Brazil was one of the greatest upsets in the history of the sport.

The 1954 World Cup was held in Switzerland, and Miguez returned to lead the title defense for Uruguay. La Celeste won the first two matches without giving up a goal and advanced to the quarterfinals against England.

The 1950 version of La Celeste, led by Óscar Miguez (squatting with hands on ball), made it two for two for Uruguay at the World Cup in Brazil

The English played a tough match, but ultimately could not defend well enough to slow down the defending champions, who won 4–2. Now if Uruguay were going to continue the streak of advancing to the final at the World Cup, they would have to get past the formidable Hungarians in the semifinals.

Hungary was the favorite to win the World Cup that year. The so-called "Golden Team" (or Aranycsapat). had not lost a match in five years—a streak of more than 30 consecutive wins. Stars Sándor Kocsis and Ferenc Puskás were two of the world's best players. Kocsis had already scored nine goals in the tournament coming into the match against Uruguay. La Celeste gave the mighty Hungarians all they could handle, scoring in the 86th minute to force extra time at 2–2. That is when Kocsis took over, scoring twice in the extra session to send Hungary through to the final. **Relegated** to the third-place game, Uruguay could not summon the will to fight against Austria and lost 3–1.

French captain Zinedine Zidane both scored a goal and received a red card in a 2006 World Cup final loss to Italy

SIDEBAR: OH SO CLOSE

Only a dozen countries in history have ever sent teams to the World Cup final match. There have been eight winners: Brazil, Germany, Italy, Argentina, Uruguay, France, England, and Spain. That means there are four countries that got as far as possible without being rewarded with the ultimate prize. Here is the list of guests at soccer's ultimate heartbreak hotel:

The Netherlands	Runner-up three times (1974, 1978, 2010)
Czechoslovakia	Runner-up twice (1934, 1962)
Hungary	Runner-up twice (1938, 1954)
Sweden	Runner-up once (1958)

Uruguay's fortunes took a dip in the next few years when it failed to qualify for the World Cup in 1958 and was eliminated in the first round in 1962. By 1966 Uruguay was playing better, making the quarterfinals in England. At the 1970 tournament in Mexico, they took it to another level.

At the 1970 World Cup, Uruguay drew into a tough group with Italy and Sweden. The only goals it scored in the group stage were against Israel in a 2–0 win. But a 0–0 draw against Italy and a 1–0 loss to Sweden were enough to get La Celeste through to the quarterfinals.

In the quarterfinals, Uruguay needed extra time to find its third goal of the tournament in a 1–0 win over Russia. In the semifinals, Uruguay was simply outmatched against a powerful Brazilian side featuring Pelé and Jairzinho, and lost 3–1 to the eventual champions. In the third-place match, Uruguay's lack of offense caught up with it in a 1–0 loss to West Germany.

That semifinal run was the last bit of success for Uruguayan soccer for a long time. The team failed to qualify for five of the next nine World Cups, and when they did qualify, were eliminated in the first round twice, never getting past the second round.

Hungary defeated Uruguay at the Stade Olympique de la Pontaise in Lausanne, Switzerland at the 1954 World Cup

Things changed in the 2010 World Cup in South Africa, thanks mostly to two men: Diego Forlán and Luis Suárez. Uruguay's two strikers had key roles in a deep run for La Celeste. Forlán scored five goals in the tournament and won the Golden Ball as best player. He was named Man of the Match three times, and Suárez twice. Suárez had three goals, but his biggest contribution came in the quarterfinals against Ghana, when he was sent off in the last minute of extra time for a deliberate handball in the penalty area, one that saved a sure goal. Ghana missed the resulting penalty kick, leading to a shootout that Uruguay won.

Without Suárez, the result in the semifinals was not as favorable, however, as Uruguay lost to the

Luis Suárez (L) and Diego Forlán were a formidable duo in the run to a 2010 World Cup semifinal. Forlán won the Golden Ball as the top player in the tournament

The Spanish and Dutch teams line up before Spain's victory in the 2010 World Cup

Netherlands 3–2. They then lost the third-place match to Germany 3–2. Forlán has retired from international play, but with stars like Suárez, Diego Godin, and Edinson Cavani, Uruguay is once again a prominent force in world soccer.

Other teams to watch in 2018 include FIFA top ten-ranked Spain, Belgium, and Portugal.

Spain has been one of the best sides in the world for several years. Nicknamed La Roja, Spain won Euro 2008 and 2012, sandwiching the 2010 World Cup championship, and was named FIFA Team of the Year six years in a row from 2008–13. With superstars like Sergio Ramos, Andrés Iniesta, David Silva, and David De Gea, Spain will be a force to reckon with in 2018.

Belgium's best World Cup result is a fourth place finish in 1986, but recent years have seen some great play from this European country. Belgium reached the quarterfinal of the Euro 2016 tournament, and in 2015 was ranked as number one in the world by FIFA, holding the top spot for four months. Now consistently in the top five, Belgium is a very real threat in 2018. Its success has been driven in large part by the emergence of midfielder Eden Hazard. At only 27 years old, Hazard is already in the top ten all-time for caps for his country at more than 80.

TOP TEAM PLAYERS TO WATCH IN RUSSIA 2018

NEYMAR (BRAZIL)
MANUEL NEUER (GERMANY)
LUIS SUÁREZ (URUGUAY)
LIONEL MESSI (ARGENTINA)
ANTOINE GRIEZMANN (FRANCE)

NEYMAR

World Cup appearances - 5

World Cup goals - 4

2nd runner up 2015 FIFA Best player in the world

2014 FIFA World Cup Dream Team

NEUER

World Cup appearances - 13

World Cup clean sheets - 8

2nd runner up 2014 FIFA Best player in the world

2014 World Cup Golden Glove winner

SUÁREZ

World Cup appearances - 8

World Cup goals - 5

4th runner up 2015 FIFA Best Player in the World

2014 Premier League Player of the Year

MESSI

World Cup appearances - 15

World Cup goals - 5

5-time winner FIFA Best player in the world

2014 FIFA World Cup Golden Ball winner

GRIEZMANN

World Cup appearances - 5

2016 La Liga Best Player

2nd runner up 2016 FIFA Best player in the world

Euro 2016 Player of the Tournament

Eden Hazard of Belgium is one of the top midfielders in the world

He helped lead Belgium to the quarterfinals of the 2014 World Cup. Hazard (who plays club soccer for Chelsea in the Premier League) has been Chelsea Player of the Year twice and Premier League Player of the Year in 2015. Recognized as one of the top players in the world, big things are expected of Hazard and Belgium in 2018.

Any squad with Cristiano Ronaldo on its roster must be taken seriously. Ronaldo led Portugal to just its second-ever World Cup semifinals appearance in 2006, but the side around him as 2018 approaches is one of the best Portugal has had in decades, consistently ranked in the top ten by FIFA. Ronaldo led Portugal to the Euro 2016 championship, and with support from players like Nani, Bruno Alves, and João Moutinho, victory in 2018 is well within reach for Portugal.

He has yet to get Portugal to a World Cup final match, but no side with superstar Cristiano Ronaldo should be discounted

TEXT-DEPENDENT QUESTIONS:

1. In which year did France win its only World Cup?
2. Which country's side was known as the "Golden Team"?
3. Which team won the Euro 2016 championship?

RESEARCH PROJECT:

Excluding current players, look up the best players in history for Belgium, Portugal, and Spain. Choose one player from each country and write a short report on them, outlining what made their careers special.

Advantage: when a player is fouled but play is allowed to continue because the team that suffered the foul is in a better position than they would have been had the referee stopped the game.

Armband: removable colored band worn around the upper arm by a team's captain, to signify that role.

Bend: skill attribute in which players strike the ball in a manner that applies spin, resulting in the flight of the ball curving, or bending, in mid-air.

Bicycle kick: a specific scoring attempt made by a player with their back to the goal. The player throws their body into the air, makes a shearing movement with the legs to get one leg in front of the other, and attempts to play the ball backwards over their own head, all before returning to the ground. Also known as an *overhead kick*.

Box: common name for the penalty area, a rectangular area measuring 44 yards (40.2 meters) by 18 yards (16.5 meters) in front of each goal. Fouls occurring within this area result in a penalty kick.

Club: collective name for a team, and the organization that runs it.

CONCACAF: acronym for the *Confederation of North, Central American and Caribbean Association Football*, the governing body of the sport in North and Central America and the Caribbean; pronounced "kon-ka-kaff."

CONMEBOL: acronym for the South American Football Association, the governing body of the sport in South America; pronounced "kon-me-bol."

Corner kick: kick taken from within a 1-yard radius of the corner flag; a method of restarting play when a player plays the ball over their own goal line without a goal being scored.

Cross: delivery of the ball into the penalty area by the attacking team, usually from the area between the penalty box and the touchline.

Dead ball: situation when the game is restarted with the ball stationary; i.e., a free kick.

Defender: one of the four main positions in soccer. Defenders are positioned in front of the goalkeeper and have the principal role of keeping the opposition away from their goal.

Dribbling: when a player runs with the ball at their feet under close control.

Flag: small rectangular flag attached to a handle, used by an assistant referee to signal that they have seen a foul or other infraction take place. "The flag is up" is a common expression for when the assistant referee has signaled for an offside.

Flick-on: when a player receives a pass from a teammate and, instead of controlling it, touches the ball with their head or foot while it is moving past them, with the intent of helping the ball reach another teammate.

Forward: one of the four main positions in football. Strikers are the players closest to the opposition goal, with the principal role of scoring goals. Also known as a *striker* or *attacker*.

Free kick: the result of a foul outside the penalty area given against the offending team. Free kicks can be either direct (shot straight toward the goal) or indirect (the ball must touch another player before a goal can be scored).

Fullback: position on either side of the defense, whose job is to try to prevent the opposing team attacking down the wings.

Full-time: the end of the game, signaled by the referees whistle. Also known as the *final whistle*.

Goal difference: net difference between goals scored and goals conceded. Used to differentiate league or group stage positions when clubs are tied on points.

Goalkeeper: one of the four main positions in soccer. This is the player closest to the goal a team is defending. They are the only player on the pitch that can handle the ball in open play, although they can only do so in the penalty area.

Goal kick: method of restarting play when the ball is played over the goal line by a player of the attacking team without a goal being scored.

Goal-line technology: video replay or sensor technology systems used to determine whether the ball has crossed the line for a goal or not.

Hat trick: when a player scores three goals in a single match.

Header: using the head as a means of playing or controlling the ball.

Linesman: another term for the assistant referee that patrols the sideline with a flag monitoring play for fouls, offsides, and out of bounds.

Long ball: attempt to distribute the ball a long distance down the field without the intention to pass it to the feet of the receiving player.

Manager: the individual in charge of the day-to-day running of the team. Duties of the manager usually include overseeing training sessions, designing tactical plays, choosing the team's formation, picking the starting eleven, and making tactical switches and substitutions during games.

Man of the Match: an award, often decided by pundits or sponsors, given to the best player in a game.

Midfielder: one of the four main positions in soccer. Midfielders are positioned between the defenders and forwards.

OFC: initials for the *Oceania Football Confederation*, the governing body of the sport in Oceania.

Offside: a player is offside if they are in their opponent's half of the field and closer to the goal line than both the second-last defender and the ball at the moment the ball is played to them by a teammate. Play is stopped and a free kick is given against the offending team.

Offside trap: defensive tactical maneuver, in which each member of a team's defense will simultaneously step forward as the ball is played forward to an opponent, in an attempt to put that opponent in an offside position.

Own goal: where a player scores a goal against their own team, usually as the result of an error.

Penalty area: rectangular area measuring 44 yards (40.2 meters) by 18 yards (16.5 meters) in front of each goal; commonly called *the box*.

Penalty kick: kick taken 12 yards (11 meters) from goal, awarded when a team commits a foul inside its own penalty area.

Penalty shootout: method of deciding a match in a knockout competition, which has ended in a draw after full-time and extra-time. Players from each side take turns to attempt to score a penalty kick against the opposition goalkeeper. Sudden death is introduced if scores are level after each side has taken five penalties.

Red card: awarded to a player for either a single serious cautionable offence or following two yellow cards. The player receiving the red card is compelled to leave the game for the rest of its duration, and that player's team is not allowed to replace him with another player. A player receiving the red card is said to have been *sent off* or *ejected*.

Side: another word for team.

Stoppage time: an additional number of minutes at the end of each half, determined by the match officials, to compensate for time lost during the game. Informally known by various names, including *injury time* and *added time*.

Striker: see Forward.

Studs: small points on the underside of a player's boots to help prevent slipping. A tackle in which a player directs their studs toward an opponent is referred to as a *studs-up challenge*, and is a foul punishable by a red card.

Substitute: a player who is brought on to the pitch during a match in exchange for a player currently in the game.

Sweeper: defender whose role is to protect the space between the goalkeeper and the rest of the defense.

Tackle: method of a player winning the ball back from an opponent, achieved either by using the feet to take possession from the opponent, or making a slide tackle to knock the ball away. A tackle in which the opposing player is kicked before the ball is punishable by either a free kick or penalty kick. Dangerous tackles may also result in a yellow or red card.

Throw-in: method of restarting play. Involves a player throwing the ball from behind a touch line after an opponent has kicked it out.

Trap: skill performed by a player, whereupon the player uses their foot (or, less commonly, their chest or thigh) to bring an airborne or falling ball under control.

UEFA: acronym for *Union of European Football Associations*, the governing body of the sport in Europe; pronounced "you-eh-fa."

Winger: wide midfield player whose primary focus is to provide crosses into the penalty area. Alternatively known as a *wide midfielder*.

World Cup: commonly refers to the men's FIFA World Cup tournament held every four years, but is also associated with the FIFA Women's World Cup, international tournaments for youth football, (such as the FIFA U-20 World Cup), and the FIFA Club World Cup.

Yellow card: shown by the referee to a player who commits a cautionable offence. If a player commits two cautionable offences in a match, they are shown a second yellow card, followed by a red card, and are then sent off. Also known as a *caution* or a *booking*.

FURTHER READING, INTERNET RESOURCES & VIDEO CREDITS:

Further Reading:

Mardona, Diego Armando. *Touched by God: How We Won the Mexico '86 World Cup*. London, England: Penguin Books, 2017.

Hurley, Michael. *World Cup Heroes (World Cup Fever)*. Hampshire, England: Raintree, 2015.

Radnedge, Keir. *World Soccer Records 2015*. London, England: Carlton Books, 2015.

Internet Resources:

FIFA: www.fifa.com

FIGC (Federazione Italiana Giuoco Calcio): http://www.figc.it/index_en.shtml

Fox Sports Soccer: http://www.foxsports.com/soccer

World Football Reference: http://fbref.com/

Video Credits:

Chapter 1:
Diego Maradona scores the Goal of the Century and the announcer loves it: *http://x-qr.net/1FzS*

Chapter 2:
Watch the highlights of the 1970 World Cup final match: *http://x-qr.net/1FHK*

Chapter 3:
Check out Gerd Müller's winning goal from the 1974 World Cup: *http://x-qr.net/1DS6*

Chapter 4:
Paolo Rossi crushes the powerful Brazilians at the 1982 World Cup: *http://x-qr.net/1FeA*

Chapter 5:
France won its first and only World Cup in 1998: *http://x-qr.net/1HG9*

INDEX

Andrew Luke

ABOUT THE AUTHOR:

Andrew Luke is a former journalist, reporting on both sports and general news for many years at television stations in various locations across the US affiliated with NBC, CBS and Fox. Prior to his journalism career he worked with the Boston Red Sox Major League baseball team. An avid writer and sports enthusiast, he has authored 26 other books on sports topics. In his downtime Andrew enjoys family time with his wife and two young children and attending hockey and baseball games in his home city of Pittsburgh, PA.

PICTURE CREDITS: